Acknowledgements

Photos: pp. 21, 25, 27 and 35 © Popperfoto,
        pp. 37 and 40 © Allsport.
Cover photo: © Stu Forster/Allsport.

Orders: please contact Bookpoint Ltd, 39 Milton Park, Abingdon, Oxon OX14 4TD. Telephone: (44) 01235 400414, Fax: (44) 01235 400454. Lines are open from 9.00–6.00, Monday to Saturday, with a 24 hour message answering service. Email address: orders@bookpoint.co.uk

British Library Cataloguing in Publication Data
A catalogue record for this title is available from The British Library

ISBN 0 340 71167 1

First published 1998
Impression number 10 9 8 7 6 5 4 3 2
Year 2003 2002 2001 2000 1999

Typeset by Fakenham Photosetting Ltd, Fakenham, Norfolk.
Printed in Great Britain for Hodder & Stoughton Educational, a division of Hodder Headline Plc, 338 Euston Road, London NW1 3BH by Redwood Books, Trowbridge, Wiltshire.

Celtic

Mike Wilson

Published in association with The Basic Skills Agency

Hodder & Stoughton

A MEMBER OF THE HODDER HEADLINE GROUP

Contents

		Page
1	A Catholic Football Team	2
2	The Old Firm	4
3	Hall of Fame	14
4	Managers	22
5	The 1990s	30

If you grow up in Glasgow,
football is religion.
And religion is football.

If you are a Catholic,
your team is Celtic.
If you are a Protestant,
your team is Rangers.

Together,
they are called 'The Old Firm'.
Always big rivals,
sometimes bitter enemies.

In Glasgow,
Rangers and Celtic
have ruled football
for over 100 years.

1 A Catholic Football Team

Glasgow Celtic FC
was the dream of one man.

He was Brother Walfrid,
a Catholic priest and teacher.
He came to Glasgow,
from County Sligo, in Ireland,
around 1870.

He worked with the poor Irish Catholics
in Glasgow's East End.

In 1887,
Hibs won the Scottish Cup Final.
Hibs were a Catholic team,
from Edinburgh.

Brother Walfrid said
Glasgow needed a Catholic football team.
Just like Edinburgh.

Celtic Football Club began life
in November 1887.

The club has always remembered
Brother Walfrid and his work.
Celtic has always worked
to help poor people,
and not just the poor Catholic families.

Brother Walfrid gave the team its name.
He wanted the name to remind people
of the links between the Celtic people
of Ireland and Scotland.

But Brother Walfrid said the name as 'Keltic',
and did so until the day he died.

It was the young Scottish players
who said the name as 'Seltic.'
And that is the way
we still say the name today.

2 The Old Firm

Celtic's very first match
was on 28 May 1888.

Guess who the other team was –
Glasgow Rangers!
In 1888,
the Rangers club was already 15 years old.

That was the start of the Old Firm.
The teams became big rivals.
And they have been big rivals,
sometimes friendly, sometimes not,
ever since.

And the score that first night?
Celtic 5, Rangers 2.

The papers said:
'Celtic FC has a bright future before it.'

How right they were!

The next year, in 1889,
Celtic got to the Final
of the Scottish Cup.

They were playing a local club,
which had been an army team.
They were called
the Third Lanark Rifle Volunteers.

The game was played in February,
in strong winds and snow.
It should have been cancelled.
The players ran onto the pitch
and all began throwing snowballs
at each other!
But the match went ahead.

Celtic lost 3–0.
They complained about the snow,
so the match was played again,
one week later.

This time Celtic did better –
they only lost 2–1!

No matter.
Celtic won the Cup a few years later –
the first of many.
They beat Queens Park 5–1 in 1892.

The Third Lanark Rifle Volunteers
disappeared.
But Celtic just went on and on,
to bigger and better things.

Brother Walfrid had wanted Celtic
to play in green.
This was to remind them
of the links with Ireland –
'the Emerald Isle'.

At first,
Celtic's shirts were white,
with green collars.
Then they tried green and white stripes.

The famous green and white hoops
came in in 1903.

In 1902,
both Celtic and Rangers took part
in the first ever British Cup.
The British Cup was a play-off between
the top two English
and top two Scottish teams.

They played against
Everton and Sunderland,
the top two teams in England
at the time.

Guess who got to the Final –
Celtic and Rangers!

The score was 2–2 at full time.
The teams didn't want to wait
for a replay on another day.
They wanted to play extra time.
So they did!

In the last few minutes,
Celtic scored the winner.
The first ever British Cup
came to Parkhead!

Rangers wanted the chance
to win the Cup back the next year.
But Celtic said they were keeping the Cup.
They had won it fair and square.
The argument went on for years.

The early 1900s
saw the best Celtic team ever.
That's what many people said.
But now,
nobody is old enough to remember!

But they did have plenty of success.
They won the League six times running.
They won the Glasgow Cup
five times out of six.
They came close to winning the Scottish Cup
three times running.
They had won it twice,
but on the third time,
there was a riot on the terraces.
The Final had to be abandoned.

It was in 1909.
Celtic were in the Scottish Cup Final
for the third year in a row.
They were playing Rangers – again.
There was always a chance of trouble
at an Old Firm game!

In the first match,
the teams drew 2–2.
60,000 fans went to the replay the next week.
The two teams drew again: 1–1.

At the end of the match,
the Celtic players waited on the pitch.
They wanted to play extra time
(and so did the fans).

But the Rangers players left the pitch.
They wanted another replay
on another day.

No-one in the crowd
knew what was happening.
The crowds began to spill onto the pitch.
One little man was dancing about,
calling for extra time.
Until somebody punched his head.

Pretty soon
there were fights everywhere.
Extra police were called,
and the fire brigade.
Grown-ups and children
were rushed to hospital.

The game was abandoned.
Nobody won the Scottish Cup that year.

In those days,
Celtic and Rangers always played
on New Year's Day.

And often,
these games led to crowd trouble.
This was because of New Year drinking.

On 1 January 1953,
Rangers won the match
at Celtic's ground, Parkhead.

The Celtic fans were not happy.
They began to throw
their empty beer bottles
at the Rangers players.

Fights broke out.
11 men were arrested.

The Scottish Football Association
wanted to make the two teams pay.
They stopped the two teams
meeting on New Year's Day.

They made Celtic build a tunnel,
to protect the players
when they came on and off the pitch.

And they told both Celtic and Rangers
to stop waving flags or colours
that might make the other side angry.

Even today,
players are told not to do anything
to make the other fans angry.

If you score a goal,
or win an Old Firm match,
you must not celebrate too much.
You must not enjoy it too much.
You might start a riot,
just like in 1953!

When Paul Gascoigne
first started playing for Rangers,
he didn't know this rule.
He scored a goal against Celtic,
then did a victory dance.
He pretended he was playing the pipes,
an old Protestant reminder
of famous battles they won over Catholics.
This was guaranteed to anger the Celtic fans!

As late as 1980,
there were still riots
between the rival fans.

In the 1980 Scottish Cup Final,
there were riots
after Celtic beat Rangers 1–0.
After the match,
drink was banned
from all Scottish football grounds.

3 Hall of Fame

There have been so many great players
to wear the famous green and white.

Here are just a few of them:

Patsy Gallagher

Patsy Gallagher
came from County Donegal,
in Ireland.

He joined Celtic, aged 17,
in 1911.

He was thin, and little,
only about 8 stones in weight.
But his speed and skill
soon made him a football legend.

He scored 184 goals for Celtic.
A lot of them were so special,
they were talked about for years.
Like the one against Hibs
in September 1921.

Hibs had just scored.
Celtic needed a quick equaliser.
Patsy got the ball
straight from the kick-off.
He ran through all of the Hibs players.
Then he carefully placed the ball
past the Hibs keeper, and in the net.

He didn't need the rest of the Celtic team!
He could just score goals on his own!

In 15 years, Patsy won
seven League Championship medals,
and 19 different Cup medals.

Before he died in 1953,
Patsy Gallagher passed his talent on:
His sons, Tommy and Willie,
both played professional football in Scotland.
(Willie Gallagher played for Celtic.)
And Patsy's grandson, Kevin Gallagher,
played for Coventry City and Scotland.

Kenny Dalglish

Kenny Dalglish was born in Glasgow
on 4 March 1951.

16 years later,
he began his football career at Celtic.

He played for Celtic for 10 years,
1967–77.
In that time,
he won four League Champions' medals
and four Cup medals.

He was brilliant at tactics.
One manager said
Kenny was always thinking
ten yards in front of all the other players.

Dalglish went on to play for Liverpool.
With them he won every big competition
south of the border.
He was even voted player of the year.

He also managed Liverpool,
and won the double.
He managed Blackburn Rovers,
when they won
the English Premier League.

Now he's with Newcastle,
planning to bring them the same success.

Charlie Nicholas

Like Kenny Dalglish,
Charlie Nicholas is home-grown talent.

He was often called Charlie Nick,
but some people called him
Bonnie Prince Charlie.
This was because he was trendy,
and good-looking.

He was also called
Champagne Charlie,
because he liked a drink or two
after a match.

He was always a cheeky player,
and a brilliant goal-scorer.

He scored two in his first game for Celtic.
All in all, he played 95 games,
and scored 79 times.
He won two League Champions' medals
and one League Cup Winners' medal.
Then he was sold,
first to Arsenal,
then to Aberdeen.

He helped Arsenal win the FA Cup
(he scored both goals
in a 2–1 win over Liverpool).

Then he helped Aberdeen
win the Cup Double
in 1989–90.
This match was against Celtic
and he scored the winning goal.
But even so, the Celtic fans
will always love Charlie Nick.

He came back to Celtic in 1990,
and scored in a 2–0 win
over Rangers in 1992.

He ended his playing days
playing for Clyde.

Charlie Nicholas.

4 Managers

When Jock Stein became manager
in 1965,
he was only the 4th manager
the club had ever had.

The first manager,
Willie Maley
had the job until 1945.
He was manager for 43 years.
(He had played for Celtic
in their first ever match,
way back in 1888.)

Then Jimmie McGrory
had the job for 20 years.

But Jock Stein was the greatest of them all.

Jock Stein played for Celtic from 1950–55.
But an ankle injury cut short
his playing career.

So he became a manager.
When he came to manage Celtic,
in 1965,
the club's next Golden Age began.

The very next season, 1966–67,
Celtic were the first team in Britain
to win the European Cup.

They beat Inter Milan 2–1
in the Final.
Three years later, in 1970,
Celtic were in the
European Cup Final again.
But this time they lost 2–1
to the Dutch team Feyenoord.

In 1975,
Jock Stein was in a car crash.
It nearly killed him.
From then on,
he was always in pain.

He went on to manage the Scotland team.
His assistant was
a young Alec Ferguson.
But his record with Celtic
was his greatest achievement.

He won the European Cup once –
one win out of two finals.

He won the League title
nine times running
(a record now copied by Rangers).

Jock Stein receives his CBE in 1970.

In those years,
Celtic got to the Scottish Cup Final
11 times, and won eight of them.

He won the Scottish League Cup
six times, out of 13 Finals.

Celtic won the Treble three times:
in 1966–67, 1968–69 and 1974–75.
(The Treble is winning the
Scottish League Championship,
Scottish Cup and Scottish League Cup
all in the same season).

In 1969, Celtic beat Rangers 4–0
in the Scottish Cup Final
to win the Treble
and round off a fantastic year!

Jock Stein got a CBE in 1970.

The Celtic team of 1968–69, with the Treble.

It was 10 September 1985.
Jock Stein was manager of Scotland.
Scotland were playing a World Cup match
against Wales.
If they won, they would be going
to the World Cup Finals.

The match was close,
all the way to the end.

At the final whistle,
Scotland had won 1–0!

The Scottish fans went wild.
Everyone was cheering
and singing 'Flower of Scotland'.

Jock Stein was everywhere,
shaking hands and hugging his players.
Suddenly he sank to the ground
and died.

The excitement was too much
for his heart.

Jock Stein's whole life –
and now his sudden death –
had been on the football field.

5 The 1990s

The 1990s have been hard for Celtic.

There have been big changes at the Club,
both on the field and off it.
And the team have not been winning
as much as they would like.

Scottish football has always been ruled
by two teams – Celtic and Rangers.
But in the 1990s,
Celtic weren't strong enough
to stand up to Rangers.

Rangers won the League
nine times in a row
(just like Celtic had done from 1966–74).
And there was nothing
Celtic could do about it.

Celtic were too busy changing and growing.
They were working hard
to become a modern side,
a successful business,
and a major international team once more.

It all started in 1992.

A business man called Fergus McCann
wanted to take over Celtic Football Club.

For 100 years,
Celtic had been run
by the same few families –
traditional, Irish families.
One of them was Patsy Gallagher's family.
One of the board members in the 1990s
was Bill Gallagher, Patsy's grandson.

He hated the new business man,
Fergus McCann,
and all he stood for.
'Traditional values are being put aside,
to make way for Celtic plc,' said Bill.
'Business men don't know
what Celtic is all about.'

The trouble was –
Celtic had no money.
There were no new players coming in,
no new blood.
The team weren't winning.
The ground was falling down.
The club was nearly bankrupt.

So much for traditional values!

By March 1994,
all the money was gone.

Celtic FC were £5 million in debt,
and the banks were ready
to close the club down.

For Celtic, the choice was simple:
sell the club to Fergus McCann,
the millionaire business man,
or die.

Fergus McCann
became Managing Director of Celtic FC
on 3 March 1994.
This was eight minutes before
the bank's deadline ran out.

Slowly but surely,
Fergus McCann dragged the club
– kicking and screaming –
into the Modern Age of Football.

But it was not always easy.
And not everyone enjoyed the trip!

The team had to move out of Celtic Park
for a year, 1994–95,
while new North and East stands were built.

Big-name strikers came and went.
Names like Van Hooijdonk,
and Di Canio.

And managers, too, came and went –
Liam Brady,
Lou Macari,
and Tommy Burns.

Celtic Park.

Sometimes it seemed
that everyone was falling out
with the new boss Fergus McCann.

But in 1995,
things began to change for the better.

27 May 1995.
Scottish Cup Final.
Celtic v Airdrie.

It might not have been the best match ever.
But Celtic fans didn't mind!
Celtic won 1–0.

It was the 30th time
they'd won the Scottish Cup.
But more importantly,
it was their first big win for six years,
since they won the double in 1988.

Celtic Football Club was
finding its feet again.
At last!

Pierre van Hooijdonk with the 1995 Scottish Cup.

When Jock Stein died in 1985,
one writer said:
He had led Celtic back to success,
after years in the shadows.
He had led the team
to 'a Paradise
that the fans must have thought
was lost forever.'

Once again,
Celtic have been in the shadows
for too long.
And other clubs
have been grabbing the limelight
that belongs at Parkhead.

Now it's time for Celtic to grab
the limelight once again.

Now there are new men
in charge at Celtic:
Jock Brown is General Manager
(he used to be a football commentator
for BBC Scotland).
And Wim Jensen is team coach
(he had been coach at Feyenoord,
the Dutch team who had beaten Celtic
in the European Cup Final
all those years ago!).

Together, they make a winning team!

As anyone at Celtic Park will tell you:
it's time to bring the glory home
to Paradise.

The Celtic squad.